The Primary Comprehension Toolkit

Strategy Book 5:
Determine Importance

Lessons

In the Toolkit, we emphasize reading to explore and learn about the world.

In this Strategy Book, the lessons for determining importance include:

Strategy Support

When we read nonfiction, we are reading to learn and remember information. Kids know how to merge their thinking with the information, and now it's time for them to figure out what makes sense to remember. We can't possibly remember every fact or piece of information, nor should we. We teach kids to tell the difference between interesting details and more important information and ideas. When kids learn to put information into their own words, they are well on their way to understanding the information and shaping it into their own thought. Kids also learn to distinguish between facts, questions, and reactions so they can sort and sift information to better organize it. They use note-taking scaffolds to hold their thinking as they prepare to share it with others.

D0503411

HEINEMANN

DEDICATED TO TEACHERS™

Copyright 2008 by Stephanie Harvey and Anne Goudvis. All rights reserved.

The authors and publisher wish to thank those who have generously given permission to reprint borrowed materials.

Library of Congress Cataloging-in-Publication Data
CIP data on file with the Library of Congress

Determine Importance
ISBN-13: 978-0-325-02152-5
ISBN-10: 0-325-02152-X

Primary Comprehension Toolkit: Language and Lessons for Active Literacy
ISBN-13: 978-0-325-00997-1
ISBN-10: 0-325-00997-X

Printed in the United States of America on acid-free paper

13   ML   5

Figure Out What's Important

Text Matters

When teaching readers how to determine important information, we choose a topic that has a few clear "big ideas" and other less important but interesting details. Our hope is that after the lesson, kids will begin to understand the difference between essential information and details. Biographies are an excellent resource for launching this strategy, because they are about people who have made contributions that supersede the interesting details of their childhoods. Although the details may have had a role in their fame, ultimately, important people are known for their lasting contributions. In other words, the details of their lives, although interesting, are not the primary reason that we remember them.

Resources & Materials

Lesson Text
TIME For Kids Bigger Picture Edition [Winter 2002] "Amazing Helen Keller" poster

Classroom Supplies
- Two-column *Interesting Details/Important Information* Anchor Chart
- A sample of a Braille text, if possible

Student Supplies
- Student copy of "Amazing Helen Keller" [See *Keep Reading! A Source Book of Short Text*, pages 13–16, or the DVD-ROM.]
- Post-its
- Pencil

Separate important information from interesting details

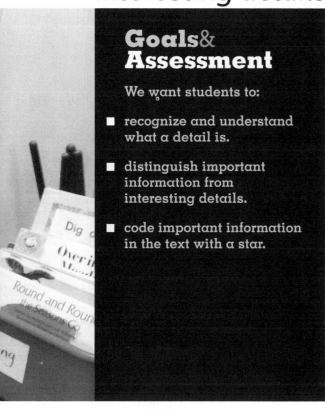

Goals& Assessment

We want students to:

- **recognize and understand what a detail is.**

- **distinguish important information from interesting details.**

- **code important information in the text with a star.**

How

Connect and Engage

- Engage kids in skimming the text and pictures of a book or article to get an idea of the contents.
- If there is an action in the book, have kids imitate or act it out.

Model

- Explain what a *detail* is.
- Model how to distinguish important information from interesting details on the Anchor Chart.

Guide

- Read a caption and ask kids what they think is most important.
- Invite kids to mark the most important information in each section with a star or asterisk.

Collaborate

- Ask kids to join a partner, read through the article one section at a time, and code the most important information in each section with a star or asterisk.
- Move around the room and confer with pairs.

Share the Learning

- Ask kids to share what they learned as well as what they think the most important information is. Add important information to the Anchor Chart.
- Invite kids to share details. Write them on the Anchor Chart.
- Wrap up by reviewing the content as well as the process that was learned and practiced in this lesson.

Why&What

We begin helping young learners to distinguish important information from less important details in the primary grades. Nonfiction is packed with information. Some of that information coalesces around a "big idea." Some of that information reveals interesting details unrelated to the bigger, more important ideas. These details, however, often capture readers by providing interesting, even quirky, information about the subject or topic at hand. Quality nonfiction brims with fascinating, yet not always salient, information. We want kids to grow up to be readers who can sift the important ideas from the interesting details but also relish that quirky information. In this lesson, we teach ways to discover the most important information so that kids can add to their knowledge base.

Lesson Text

The *TIME For Kids* "Amazing Helen Keller" poster examines the life of an extraordinary woman through fascinating photos, captions, and other text features. This piece gives kids many opportunities to root out the difference between interesting tidbits and ideas that are more important. This *TFK* poster includes a number of details that, although interesting, are not very important in the grand scheme of things. We understand that Helen Keller is renowned for her many accomplishments, despite her disabilities, and we want kids to understand that above all. Using the article, kids can practice how to sift the important ideas about Helen Keller from the details.

Used with permission from *Time For Kids.*

TEACHING MOVES   **TEACHING LANGUAGE**

Connect and Engage

Engage kids in skimming the text and pictures of a book or article to get an idea of the contents.

[I pass out individual copies of the "Amazing Helen Keller" article.] Look at this article about a very famous person called Helen Keller. You may have heard of her before. Scan the pictures and skim the words to get an idea about her. When I say scan and skim, I mean look over the pages. Don't try to read it all. Take a look at the title, the photographs, and the captions. *[Kids skim article.]* Turn to each other and talk about what you learned about Helen Keller from looking at the article. *[Kids turn and talk for a half a minute or so as I crouch down and listen in. Then I turn to the group.]* Who has some thoughts?

Tori: She couldn't hear.

Josh: And she couldn't see.

That's right. It even says that right here under the title: *Amazing Helen Keller. She was blind and deaf, but that did not stop Helen Keller from doing great things!* Imagine that. Not being able to hear or see. However, it sounds like she didn't give up even though she couldn't see or hear.

If there is an action in the book, have kids imitate or act it out.

Jana: I found something on the back page. It shows sign language.

Good noticing, Jana. How many of you noticed that? Let's look at the back page. Figure out how it works. Maybe you can spell something with your hands in sign language. Try spelling your name with a partner. *[Kids become totally engrossed in making letters in sign language and attempting to spell their names. After a few minutes, I call them back together.]*

How many of you figured out how to spell your name? Sign language is one way people who are deaf communicate. Helen Keller was deaf. She couldn't see, either. I wonder how she communicated with people, being deaf and blind. Let's read some of this article and find out more about this amazing person.

Model

When writers write nonfiction, they include a lot of details to make the writing interesting. A detail is a little bit of information about something. When writers write about a famous person, as this writer did, they usually include details, such as when the person was born, what the person looked like, and things such as that. These details make the article more interesting, but the details are not the most important information. For instance, if I say, "Jack is one of the kindest people I know. He always goes out of his way to help people. His shoes are brand-new." Which is the most important information and which is a detail? Turn to each other and talk. *[Kids turn and talk.]*

> Mica: That he is really nice to people and helps them out is the most important.

I agree; that part is more important than his new shoes. His new shoes are a detail, aren't they?

When we are learning about something, we can't remember all of the information that we come across. We have to try to figure out what information is the most important. We have to try to separate the interesting details from the more important ideas—because we want to remember the important information. Let me show you how it works. *[I point to the* Interesting Details/Important Information *Anchor Chart.]* I have this two-column Anchor Chart entitled *Interesting Details/Important Information.* This article is full of photos of Helen Keller at different times of her life. I am going to read the beginning of the article and show you how I decide which information is a detail and which is a more important idea. I will jot the detail in the *Interesting Details* column and the important information in the *Important Information* column.

[I read the beginning of the article.]

Helen Keller was born more than 120 years ago. She became blind and deaf when she was just a baby. A special teacher helped her learn to read and speak. Helen did not let anything stand in her way!

OK, let me think this through. *Helen Keller was born more than 120 years ago.* Hmmm, that's a long time ago, but I am not sure that is the most important idea. I think that is more of an interesting detail. Being blind and deaf is important information about Helen Keller, because that is one of the things we remember about her, not when she was born, but that she was blind and deaf and never let it stand in her way. That is definitely important! So I am going to write *Born 120 years ago* in the *Interesting Details* column and *Helen Keller was blind and deaf, but she didn't let anything stand in her way* in the *Important Information* column. Does this make some sense? *[Kids nod.]*

Turn to each other and talk about the difference between interesting details and important information. *[Kids turn and talk.]*

Explain what a *detail* is.

Model how to distinguish important information from interesting details on the Anchor Chart.

Interesting Details	Important Information
• Born 120 years ago	• Helen Keller was blind and deaf, but she didn't let anything stand in her way.

Guide

Read a caption and ask kids what they think is most important.

Let's try sorting together. Look at this photo of Helen when she was 39 years old. The caption says: *Helen loved horseback riding. She believed that blind and deaf people could do almost anything.* Turn to each other and talk about what you think the most important information is. *[Kids turn and talk as I crouch down and listen to them. Most seem to separate the more important information from the details.]* What do you think?

Ellie: Most important is that she believed blind and deaf people could do almost anything.

What makes you think that, Ellie?

Ellie: If blind and deaf people think they can do anything, they will have a much better life.

Such deep thinking, Ellie. Did everyone hear what Ellie said? Say it once more, will you, Ellie? What you said is so important. *[Ellie repeats her statement.]*

Thanks, Ellie. Very thoughtful. So, what is the detail here?

Erik: That she loved to ride horses.

Exactly, Erik.

Veronique: But I love horses, too. They are really important to me.

Such a good point, Veronique. Sometimes, we connect the details to our own lives, like you just did. In fact, Helen's being able to ride a horse shows that she could do almost anything. So horseback riding is a detail here, but it has to do with a big, important idea. That's how details work sometimes; they give us more information about what is important. So let's record this detail and the important information on the Anchor Chart.

Interesting Details

- Born 120 years ago

- She loved riding horses.

Important Information

- Helen Keller was blind and deaf, but she didn't let anything stand in her way.

- She believed deaf and blind people could do almost anything.

I have an idea. I am going to put a star right on a Post-it next to the most important information in the caption of this photograph. A star is a code we can use to show that something is important. Kids in high school and college code important information with a star. Why wait for college? Let's start coding important information with a star right now! *[I hand out Post-its and pencils, then show kids how to draw a star (or an asterisk if they are not yet able to draw a star). I give them a little time to practice drawing them.]*

OK, I am going to draw a star on a Post-it and put it right next to the part of the caption that says *She believed that blind and deaf people could do almost anything* since I think that is really important. I may draw a picture or write a few words about what I think is important, too. If you agree that sentence is the most important information in this part, go ahead and mark it with a star. *[Kids draw a star on a Post-it and put it next to that part of the text.]*

Invite kids to mark the most important information in each section with a star or asterisk.

TIP: Some younger kids are unable to draw stars. The purpose of text coding is to quickly note information, not to struggle with the art. So we model how to make a star as well as an asterisk (*) which merely involves drawing three intersecting lines. Kids can choose! But if some spend undue amounts of time working on their stars, we nudge them to code with an asterisk instead.

An Amazing Life

Helen Keller was born more than 120 years ago. She became blind and deaf when she was just a baby. A special teacher helped her learn to read and speak. Helen Keller did not let anything stand in her way!

Age 7

Helen had no way to speak until she was 7. Then she began to learn sign language.

Age 19

Annie Sullivan taught Helen to spell words with her hands. She even went to college with Helen.

Age 39

Helen loved horseback riding. She believed that blind and deaf people could do almost anything.

Collaborate

Ask kids to join a partner, read through the article one section at a time, and code the most important information in each section with a star or asterisk.

Move around the room and confer with pairs.

TIP: When you have kids read together as partners, you can decide how to set up those partnerships. They can be random or assigned. There is only one requirement: At least one of the partners must be able to read the information if there is text. Additionally, we let listeners know that they have the biggest job, to listen and think about what the reader is reading and then to talk to the reader about it. That way both partners are engaged in active literacy.

OK, now you get a chance to try this. Find a partner and go through the article together. Talk about what you think is most important and code it with a star or asterisk. You don't have to agree, but make sure you discuss it, because talking to each other can really help us decide whether something is important or not. Go ahead. Enjoy! *[I give kids a couple of minutes to get started, and then I begin conferring with pairs.]*

So how is it going, you two?

Brandy: Look at this picture of Helen on the horse. Her eyes are open.

So they are.

Michelle: But she is blind. That's important, we think.

Talk more about that.

Michelle: Well, we never knew that you could have your eyes open and still be blind.

Brandy: I thought if you were blind, your eyes would have to be closed, but now I know that isn't true.

Interesting. So, that is new information for you?

Brandy and Michelle: Yes.

Sometimes when we learn something new, it becomes important to us because we never knew it before. I have a question for you. Do you think the fact that she has her eyes open could be a detail? Remember, we learned that details give us a little bit of interesting information.

Michelle: It's a detail. But it is really interesting.

Details usually are interesting bits of information. What do you think is most important here?

Brandy: That she could do almost anything.

Good thinking!

[I move on to Marc and Davis who are poring over the photo of the Braille alphabet.]

Hi, you two. What's going on?

Davis: How can she read this if she can't see it?

Such a good question. You see those little dots; they are actually little bumps on the paper, so you don't have to be able to see them. You read the letters by feeling the bumps, which is what Helen is doing in the photograph, although it is kind of hard to tell that. I'll try to find a Braille book for you, which is a book written with those little bumps so that blind people can read. It will give you a much better idea of how Helen read. Either of you want to read this caption?

Marc: Sure. "She helped other blind and deaf people learn to read. Here she is with an alphabet for the blind."

What is most important, do you think? Where would you draw your star?

Davis: That she helped other blind and deaf people learn to read. That is really amazing because she couldn't see or hear.

I so agree with you. Amazing and very important. Would you guys be willing to share this thinking during our sharing circle? *[Marc and Davis nod and I move on to confer with other pairs. I check in with Jessica and Jeremy.]*

Jessica: I found something really important. Helen Keller met a lot of presidents.

Jeremy: Twelve presidents!

She did, didn't she? Why do you suppose she got to meet all of those presidents?

Jessica: Because she was famous.

So interesting. Why was she famous?

Jeremy: Because she did a lot of things, even though she was blind and deaf. She even went to college and wrote books.

So, I have a question: Was the most important thing about her that she met the presidents?

Jessica: Most important is that she did so many things and worked so hard.

I think so. As a matter of fact, she probably got to meet those presidents because she did so many amazing things and worked so hard, even though she was blind and deaf.

Jeremy: But it would still be really cool to meet the president!

I can't argue with that, Jeremy. Good thinking, you two.

Share the Learning

I'm going to invite Marc and Davis to share what they learned. Marc and Davis, would you like to share what you learned and what you think is important?

Marc and Davis: Yes, thank you.

Marc: We learned that if you are blind, you read from a special book that has bumps that you can feel. You read by touching the book.

Davis: We think the most important thing is that Helen taught other deaf and blind people to read. That is amazing. We wonder how she could do that— teach people to read when she couldn't see or hear.

[If I have a sample of Braille text, I pass it around for kids to feel.] So interesting. You picked out such important information: that Helen taught others to read. And you wonder how she was able to do that. I wonder that, too. I think a lot of people wonder that. Sometimes when we learn new important information, we have a question about it, don't we? Maybe we could do some research to find out more about that. In the meantime, let's add that important information to the Anchor Chart. *[I write on the Anchor Chart: She taught other deaf and blind people to read.]*

Did anyone find a detail?

Brandy and Michelle: We did.

Ask kids to share what they learned as well as what they think the most important information is. Add important information to the Anchor Chart.

Remind us what a detail is and then share yours.

Michelle: A detail is a little bit of information that is kind of interesting.

Brandy: And maybe not so important.

Such good thinking! Can you share a detail you found?

Brandy: *[Points to the photo of Helen Keller horseback riding.]* Right here, Helen's eyes are open, but she is blind. We never knew that. We thought if you are blind, you have your eyes closed. That's a detail.

It certainly is. You picked up that detail from looking at the picture. Some details are in the text and some come from looking at the pictures. Remember, details give a little bit of information that often makes the topic more interesting. Let's add that detail to the Anchor Chart in the *Interesting Details* column. *[I write* Her eyes are open but she is blind *on the Anchor Chart.]*

You all did a wonderful job with this today. First of all, you learned a lot about an important figure in history. Helen Keller was unique in all the world for the reasons that you discovered today. She believed that deaf and blind people could do almost anything, and she proved it by the life she led. It is not surprising that the article is entitled "Amazing Helen Keller." She was truly amazing. And now you know so much about her.

You also worked on picking out the most important information, which is such a special thing to be able to do! And you learned what a detail is: a small bit of information. In the next few days, you can try this with your own books. You can draw a star or asterisk on a small Post-it since we can't write in the books. Then you can put it next to the most important part that you read or see. Great work today.

Interesting Details	Important Information
• Born 120 years ago	• Helen Keller was blind and deaf, but she didn't let anything stand in her way.
• She loved riding horses.	• She believed deaf and blind people could do almost anything.
• Her eyes are open but she is blind.	• She taught other deaf and blind people to read.

Did your students:

- recognize and understand what a detail is?

- distinguish important information from interesting details?

- code important information in the text with a star?

Reflect& Assess

When we first introduce determining importance to young kids, we expect that they will need some time before they are really adept at separating the important ideas from the interesting details. The story of Helen Keller is a terrific one to launch determining importance because she was such a remarkable human being and she did some very important things. Most of the assessment in this lesson is in the form of oral conversation about Helen Keller. The *Collaborate* and *Share the Learning* sections show how we confer with kids to help them sift details from important ideas. Brandy and Michelle were fascinated with the fact that Helen had her eyes open while riding a horse. They couldn't stop thinking about the fact that she was blind but her eyes were open. That conference shows one way that we can help kids sort the bigger ideas from the details. Because the kids in this lesson were kindergarteners, in most cases we had to talk to them about what was most important and why. Some got the big ideas like the fact that she could do almost anything even though she was deaf and blind. One suggested that we all could learn from her. It is through oral conversation that kids begin to understand the difference between a detail and a more important idea.

Adapt& Differentiate

This lesson was done with kindergarteners, but here are suggestions for how to adapt and differentiate for the whole range of learners.

During collaborative practice, kids work together to put their Post-its marked with stars next to the most important information. Some kids put a star only, and others draw or jot down a thought about why it is an important part. Some kids, particularly younger children, can't yet draw stars, so we model how to draw an asterisk (*) instead. This lesson fosters a rich discussion, which sparks most of the learning. We ask questions that will mine nuggets—questions such as "What makes you think that?" "How did you come up with that?" and "Can you say more about that?" We also read and look at kids' Post-its. In many cases, we confer with kids to understand what they are thinking, particularly when they draw or use very early invented spelling. Older kids, second graders, and more developed readers are likely to write more and draw more explicitly. When they go off to work together, one partner must be able to read the material if there is text reading involved. Large photographs and images work well for younger kids who cannot yet read words.

Post-its that Demonstrate Understanding of Some Important Ideas

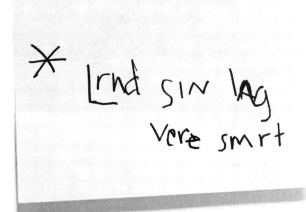

1 "Helen could read and write but could not see and hear." This student went straight to one of the most important ideas in the piece. She separated a big important idea from the many details.

2 "Helen learned sign language. She was very smart." This student got close to an important idea. The sign language is more of a detail, but the student picked up on Helen's intelligence, which is central in her accomplishments.

3 Sophie dictated this response. Although she didn't write or draw, Sophie hit on the most important idea, which she expressed through talking.

Post-its that Require Further Investigation

4 Sam drew Helen riding a horse. He dictated that Helen liked to ride horses even though she couldn't see or hear. Sam is right, but I confer with him and we talk about bravery, a more important idea than merely liking to ride.

5 This student was excited about Helen Keller meeting so many presidents. I confer with her to get a handle on why this is important, why Helen got to meet so many presidents.

6 This student referred to Anne Sullivan. It makes perfect sense that he thought she was a nice teacher, because the text says Anne taught Helen to spell with her hands and even went to college with her. I confer with the student to tease out a bigger idea about Anne—about the importance of education rather than merely the idea that she was nice.

Lesson (16) Guide

This Lesson Guide can help you teach students to separate important information from interesting details, using any text of your choice.

Figure Out What's Important

Separate important information from interesting details

TEACHING MOVES	TEACHING LANGUAGE
	Connect and Engage
Engage kids in skimming the text and pictures of a book or article to get an idea of the contents.	■ Look at this article about…. Scan the pictures and skim the words to get an idea about…. Turn to each other and talk about what you learned about…from looking through the text.
If there is an action in the book, have kids imitate or act it out.	■ Let's look at this page and see how we could act out this part.
	Model
Explain what a *detail* is.	■ In nonfiction, writers use a lot of details to make the writing interesting. A *detail* is a little bit of information about something.
Model how to distinguish important information from interesting details on the Anchor Chart.	■ We can't always remember all the information we come across when we read. So we have to separate the interesting details from the important information. We want to remember the important information.
	■ As I read this article, watch how I decide which information is a detail and which is a more important idea. I will jot the detail in the *Interesting Details* column and the important information in the *Important Information* column of this Anchor Chart.
	Guide
Read a caption and ask kids what they think is most important.	■ Let's try sorting some information together. Look at this photograph and the caption for it. Turn to each other and talk about what you think the important information is.
Invite kids to mark the most important information in each section with a star or asterisk.	■ A star is a code we can use to show that something is important. I am going to put a star on a Post-it and place it next to the most important information in the section. If you agree that this is important information, you can mark your Post-it with a star and place it right next to the important information.

The Teaching Moves outline your instructional sequence and the
Teaching Language gives you an idea about what to say to your students.

TEACHING LANGUAGE	TEACHING MOVES

Collaborate

- Find a partner and go through the article together. Talk about what you think is most important. You may not agree, but your discussion can help you as you make your decision.

  Ask kids to join a partner, read through the article one section at a time, and code the most important information with a star or asterisk.

- As you work together, I will walk around and see if you need any help. How's it going, you two? Talk more about that…. What do you think is most important here?

  Move around the room and confer with pairs.

Share the Learning

- I'm going to invite…to share what they learned. Would you like to share what you learned and what you think is important? So interesting. You picked out such important information. Let's add that to our chart.

  Ask kids to share what they learned as well as what they think the most important information is. Add important information to the Anchor Chart.

- Did anyone find a detail? Such good thinking. Remind us what a detail is and then share yours. Let's add that detail to the chart.

  Invite kids to share details. Write them on the Anchor Chart.

- You worked on picking out the most important information, and you learned what a detail is: a small bit of information. Now you can try this in your own books. Great work today!

  Wrap up by reviewing the content as well as the process that was learned and practiced in this lesson.

Reflect & Assess

Did your students:

- recognize and understand what a detail is?
- distinguish important information from interesting details?
- code important information in the text with a star?

Paraphrase Information

Text Matters

Accessible, interesting texts with lots of features support kids as they learn to paraphrase. Initially, we choose texts that are brief and to the point so that kids aren't lost in a sea of information. We work with sections of the text—short paragraphs or pictures with captions—to begin teaching the process. As kids gain skill in putting information in their own words, we give them longer and more complex text to tackle. When kids have background knowledge about a topic, we encourage them to add their thoughts to the mix.

Resources&Materials

Lesson Text
TIME For Kids Bigger Picture Edition [April 2002] "A Visit to Mexico" poster

Additional Texts
A variety of nonfiction magazines and books

Classroom Supplies
- *Steps for Paraphrasing* Anchor Chart
- *Paraphrasing* Anchor Chart
- Clipboard
- Post-its

Student Supplies
- Student copy of "A Visit to Mexico" [See *Keep Reading! A Source Book of Short Text*, pages 17–19, or the DVD-ROM.]
- Post-its
- Pencil

Merge your thinking to make meaning

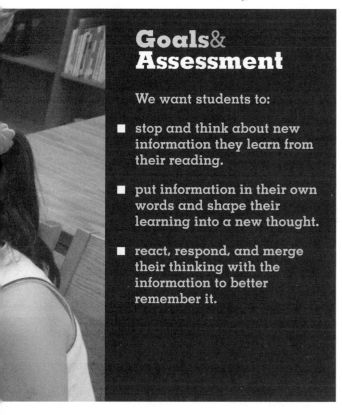

Goals & Assessment

We want students to:

- stop and think about new information they learn from their reading.

- put information in their own words and shape their learning into a new thought.

- react, respond, and merge their thinking with the information to better remember it.

Why & What

Young kids love to talk about and respond to what they are learning. This lesson teaches kids to paraphrase so they can accurately remember the important knowledge they gain. It builds on earlier lessons by asking kids to put information into their own words after they have stopped to think about it. Kids say the information to themselves in a way that makes sense. They turn and talk with someone else, emphasizing what they think is important. Once kids have put the information in their own words, we ask them to react, respond, and merge their thinking with the information. When kids shape their learning into a new thought, they are much more likely to understand and remember it.

How

Connect and Engage

- Review that when learners read for information, they read, stop, and think about it.
- Reiterate some of the strategies kids use to get information from photographs.
- Remind kids to pay special attention to the nonfiction features.

Model

- Introduce and define the term *paraphrase*.
- List the steps of paraphrasing information.
- Model how to paraphrase and record your thinking, merging your thinking with the information.

Guide

- Continue reading, and then ask kids to turn and talk to try to put the information in their own words.
- Invite kids to share out their thinking and record it on the Anchor Chart.
- Expand on a comment from one child to show how to merge thinking with the information and paraphrase.

Collaborate or Practice Independently

- Send kids off to read and put information into their own words, reminding them to look at the chart if they need guidance.
- Confer with kids to make sure they have accurate information and are merging their thinking with the information.

Share the Learning

- Invite kids who selected the lesson text and other nonfiction text to share their experience with paraphrasing and adding personal reactions.
- Wrap up the lesson and remind children to use the Anchor Chart as a guide to paraphrasing information.

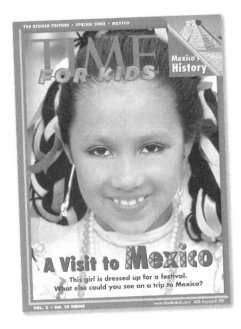

Used with permission from *Time For Kids*.

Lesson Text

The *TIME For Kids* "A Visit to Mexico" poster is full of photographs with short captions, just right for kids learning to paraphrase. Most of the information is quite general, so kids have some latitude for putting the information in their own words in a way that makes sense to them. Once they understand the information on the page, kids who have some background knowledge can add what they know about Mexico—merging their thinking with the information from the poster. We encourage kids to react and respond to information in a variety of ways, whether they have background knowledge about it or not.

TEACHING MOVES　　　**TEACHING LANGUAGE**

Connect and Engage

Review that when learners read for information, they read, stop, and think about it.

[I hold up the "A Visit to Mexico" poster unfolded to show many images of the country.] Look at the pictures on this poster. It's all about Mexico. As we look at the pictures, let's remember that one of the best ways to learn new information is to look carefully, stop for a moment, and think about it. You have been doing some great thinking as you read. You have noticed new learning, activated your background knowledge, and asked thoughtful questions. All these strategies help us better understand the information we're viewing, listening to, and reading. Today we are going to think about new information and put it into our own words so we really understand it.

So, let's "read" the photographs up here on the poster. We'll stop to think and look carefully at them. When we view photographs carefully, we are using our minds to think about the information, just like when we are reading. Take a minute and stop and think about what you see. Then turn and talk about what you observe or have learned from these pictures.

John: I see the Mexican flag. I know it has an eagle on it.

Aracelli: That big building is the capital of Mexico because it has the flag of Mexico.

Gina: There is a map. I noticed on the map that Mexico is right next to the United States.

Jared: I noticed a woman dancing. I wonder if it's Cinco de Mayo.

Reiterate some of the strategies kids use to get information from photographs.

Notice that you are using thinking strategies to gain accurate information from these photographs. You looked carefully at the photographs and learned some facts from them. You activated your background knowledge and made connections to the information in the pictures. Aracelli inferred that the big building in the photo is the capital of Mexico because she noticed the

Mexican flag flying there. The poster says that Mexico City is the capital of Mexico—just like you were thinking, Aracelli. Jared noticed a woman dancing and asked about it. John knew there is an eagle on the Mexican flag. You are already talking about the information in your own words and merging your thinking with it.

Another thing you did was pay attention to visual features, like this map. The title of this two-page spread is "Our Neighbor." As Gina noticed, Mexico is right next to the United States. Let's read and see what else we can learn. *[I read the part under the title.]*

Remind kids to pay special attention to the nonfiction features.

Our Neighbor

Mexico is our neighbor. It is the sunny country south of the United States. Mexico is famous for its music, art, food, native people, and more!

That information confirms what Gina told us—that Mexico is right next to the United States. We learned that Mexico is a country with a rich culture—music, art, food, and interesting people.

Model

Let me start by reading the caption that goes with the photograph of the kids who are sitting on top of some old ruins. *[I read.]*

Mexico has pyramids. They were made by people who lived there thousands of years ago.

These are pyramids that were built a long time ago. I'm going to paraphrase the information I read here. When I paraphrase, I read the information, stop to think about it, and say what I learned in my own words. We are much more likely to understand what we read when we put the information into our own words.

Introduce and define the term *paraphrase*.

I've written the steps I will use to paraphrase on this Anchor Chart. *[I point to the chart as I read the steps.]*

List the steps of paraphrasing information.

Steps for Paraphrasing Information

- Read the information, stop, and think about it.

- Say the information in my own words but don't say too much.

- React and respond to the information, merging my thinking with it.

Model how to paraphrase and record your thinking, merging your thinking with the information.

I'll write the information from the poster in the left column. Now I'm going to think about the information in order to put it in my own words and I won't say too much. I'll say, "Mexican pyramids were built by people who lived a very long time ago." Notice that I didn't tell too much, did I? Now I'm going to look at the photograph that goes with the caption. I have a response. I see the modern kids sitting high up on the pyramids, and I'm amazed that pyramids that are so old are still there! I'll say, "I'm amazed such old pyramids have lasted so long!" I merged some of my thinking with what I noticed in the picture. I'll write this on our Anchor Chart, too.

Notice I wrote the words from the text in the left-hand column, and my own words in the right-hand column.

Let's see if I followed the steps we talked about. I read and then stopped to think about the information. I put the information I got from the caption and the photograph in my own words. And then I merged my thinking with the information; I added some of my own thinking.

TIP: When first introducing paraphrasing, I write the actual text in the left column and show how I put the facts into my own words in the right column. This makes the distinction very clear to kids.

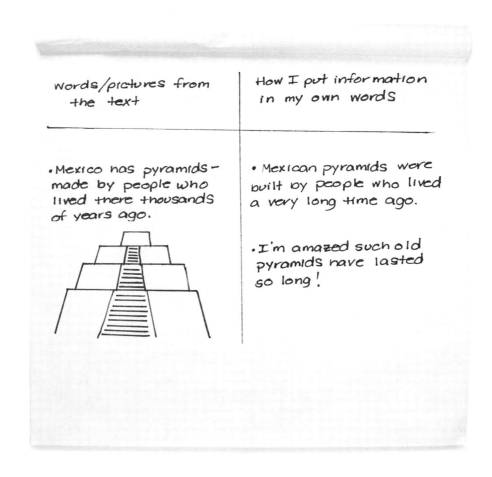

words/pictures from the text	How I put information in my own words
• Mexico has pyramids — made by people who lived there thousands of years ago.	• Mexican pyramids were built by people who lived a very long time ago.
	• I'm amazed such old pyramids have lasted so long!

Guide

[I hand out Post-its and pencils.] OK, now it's your turn. Let's see if we can read and think about another caption and photograph, and then put the information in our own words. Jared got us started with this photograph of the woman dancing. He wondered if it's about the Cinco de Mayo holiday. Let's check it out.

> *Mexico has colorful festivals and holidays. People dress up, dance, and sing for Cinco de Mayo.*

Jared is on the right track. The caption mentions Cinco de Mayo. That's Spanish for May 5. And on that day, there are lots of celebrations. People celebrate the day when Mexico won an important battle over the French. It's become a popular holiday in the United States, too.

Now I'd like you to turn and talk with a partner to put this information in your own words and add your thinking to it. Let's look back at our chart of steps to help you remember what to do. Stop and think about the information, put what's important into your own words, and then merge your thinking with it. We'll share out in a minute. *[Kids turn and talk. I listen in and write down kids' thinking, capturing their words. Or I encourage them to write and/or draw their thinking on Post-its themselves.]*

Let's come back together. Take a look at our Anchor Chart. I've written words from the poster in the left-hand column. As you share, I will write the information you paraphrase in the right-hand column. Would you like to share, Max?

> Max: Yes, thank you. I know that in Mexico they celebrate Cinco de Mayo with dancing, games, and food.

You paraphrased the information about dancing on Cinco de Mayo, and then you added your thinking—that games and food are part of the celebration. I'll jot that down.

> Arianna: On Cinco de Mayo, mariachis play music and people dance!

So great, you are putting important information from the caption and photo in your own words, Arianna. I see you have written some of your thinking on a Post-it. Good for you! I'll write what you said up on our chart, too.

Continue reading, and then ask kids to turn and talk to try to put the information in their own words.

Invite kids to share out their thinking and record it on the Anchor Chart.

words/pictures from the text	How I put information in my own words
• Mexico has pyramids—made by people who lived there thousands of years ago. 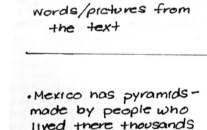	• Mexican pyramids were built by people who lived a very long time ago. • I'm amazed such old pyramids have lasted so long!
• Mexico has colorful festivals and holidays. People dress up, dance, and sing for Cinco de Mayo.	• In Mexico, they celebrate Cinco de Mayo with dancing, games, and food. • Mariachis play music and people dance!

Expand on a comment from one child to show how to merge thinking with the information and paraphrase.

Celia: Another holiday is the Day of the Dead.

Tell us some more about the Day of the Dead, Celia.

Celia: They think about the people in their families that died on the Day of the Dead. In our class we brought in pictures of a grandma or a grandpa who died. Then we put food and flowers by the pictures.

That's an important connection you've made, Celia. Your experience with this day helps you understand another important celebration in Mexico. We could say, "On the Day of the Dead, they remember people in their family who have died." *[I write on the Anchor Chart.]* From reading and merging our thinking with the information, we've learned that holidays and celebrations are important to people in Mexico. I'll add that to the chart, too.

words/pictures from the text	How I put information in my own words
• Mexico has pyramids — made by people who lived there thousands of years ago. 	• Mexican pyramids were built by people who lived a very long time ago.
	• I'm amazed such old pyramids have lasted so long!
• Mexico has colorful festivals and holidays. People dress up, dance, and sing for Cinco de Mayo.	• In Mexico, they celebrate Cinco de Mayo with dancing, games, and food.
	• Mariachis play music and people dance!
	• On the Day of the Dead, they remember people in their family who have died.
	• Holidays and celebrations are important to people in Mexico.

Collaborate or Practice Independently

You've done a great job of viewing, listening, thinking, and putting the information in your own words. Now you are going to try this on your own. *[I hand out Post-its, pencils, and copies of the student version of "A Visit to Mexico."]* You are welcome to use "A Visit to Mexico," or you can choose a book you would like to read from the book baskets on the tables. Make sure you have some Post-its with you, and you can begin reading. When you come to some important information or a picture that teaches you some information, remember to stop and think about the information, put it in your own words, don't say too much, and add your response or reaction if you like. Look up at the steps on the chart if you need a reminder about what to do. You are welcome to work by yourself or with a partner. I will come around to confer with you as you read. I'm excited about seeing all the new learning that's going to happen!

> *[I stop to confer with Jaime and Lizette.]*
>
> How's it going? Will you read me what you were just writing?
>
> Jaime: *[reads from his Post-its]* I know that the Aztecs made pyramids a long time ago. It took them a long time to build it, but they built it.

That's so interesting, Jaime. You took information from the poster about the pyramids and then you added your thinking. You have some accurate information about the Aztecs, who were people who lived a long time ago in Mexico. And you drew the Aztecs building the pyramids, too.

> Lizette: *[reads from her Post-its]* I know that a long time ago Aztecs made pyramids. I know that pyramids are big.

You both put what you learned into your own words and added your thinking to shape the information into a new thought. We're going to share now; will you both share what you know about the Aztecs? You can teach the whole class this important information.

Send kids off to read and put information into their own words, reminding them to look at the chart if they need guidance.

Confer with kids to make sure they have accurate information and are merging their thinking with the information.

Share the Learning

Is there anyone who read another nonfiction book who would like to share? *[Joel and Ella raise their hands.]*

> Joel and Ella, would you like to share?
>
> Ella: We read about owls.

Would you read the words in your text, please? Look everyone, here's a big picture of an owl.

> Joel *[reads]*: Owls are on the lookout at night. Their big eyes shine. I wrote, "Owls are awake at night. They are looking for food to eat. They are hunters."
>
> Ella: I wrote, "I think the owl is looking for mice to eat!"

Invite kids who selected the lesson text and other nonfiction text to share their experience with paraphrasing and adding personal reactions.

You two really thought about the information. You inferred that being "on the lookout" meant the owls were awake, looking for food and hunting. Great job of paraphrasing these facts about owls, Joel! And you made an interesting inference, too, Ella. You said "I think..."

Ella: I don't know for sure, but I think owls eat mice, so that's why I said "I think."

So thoughtful. That's something else we have learned to do, isn't it? It's a good idea to use the words "I think" or "I infer" when we think we know some information but need to check it out. I'll be interested to see what you find out! Both of you put the information you were reading into your own words and shaped your learning into a new thought.

Now I'd like to ask Jaime and Lizette to share their thinking about this article.

Lizette: I know that a long time ago Aztecs made pyramids. I know that pyramids are big.

And Jaime—it's your turn.

Jaime: I know the Aztecs made pyramids a long time ago, and it took them a long time to build them.

Jaime and Lizette taught us such interesting information! That's a good reason to paraphrase information, so we can teach it to others.

You have done a fine job of reading and viewing to learn new information and then put it into your own words. I'm looking forward to conferring with you as you keep paraphrasing your learning to really understand it! Remember to look back at the Anchor Chart so you know what to do!

Wrap up the lesson and remind children to use the Anchor Chart as a guide to paraphrasing information.

TIP: When kids, especially English Language Learners, are reticent to share, we help them rehearse their thinking as I did in the earlier conferences. This supports them to speak out in the large group.

Did your students:

- stop and think about new information they learned from their reading?

- put information in their own words and shape their learning into a new thought?

- react, respond, and merge their thinking with the information to better remember it?

Reflect& Assess

Getting kids in the habit of paraphrasing when they are in the primary grades is plagiarism prevention for the future! When kids read, stop to think about the information, and say it to themselves in a way that makes sense, they are less likely to become what might be called "overly text dependent." Young children seem to have little difficulty putting information in their own words, so we emphasize paraphrasing early and often!

The last thing we want kids to do is forsake their authentic kid-like voices as they paraphrase information. So when we assess kids' responses and notes, we first check to see that they are not just parroting back what the text says. Then we make sure kids have written and drawn information that is clear and under-standable—but that sounds like them, not an encyclopedia!

Adapt& Differentiate

This lesson was done with first graders, but here are suggestions for how to adapt and differentiate for the whole range of learners.

With a sophisticated task like paraphrasing, it makes sense to start small. So for kindergarteners, we would take a very simple text, read it and view the pictures, and ask kids to talk about what they heard, emphasizing what they heard without saying too much. For an emergent reader, paraphrasing can be a simple sentence that describes a picture. The more accessible the text, the better the chance that kids will merge their thinking with the information to shape it into a new thought.

Our long-term goal is for kids to use paraphrasing as part of their own research. With more experienced readers, we often provide a few paragraphs of text and ask them to paraphrase the information in the margins, right next to the text. The goal is to understand what's in the text, merge our thinking with it, and shape the information in a new thought, so we discourage rote recall of information.

Guided Practice Post-its

1 I look for evidence that kids continue to use strategies taught previously. Ariana, a child learning English, used language demonstrating her connection to information about Cinco de Mayo. This is evidence that Ariana activated her background knowledge and merged her thinking with the information.

"This reminds me of my aunt that she dances in the party of Cinco de Mayo."

"Why does the Mexican flag have an eagle?"

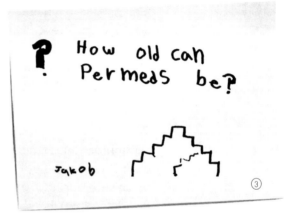

"How old can pyramids be?"

2 and 3 Jakob asked questions about information on the *TFK* poster. This demonstrates that he is continuing to use questioning strategies taught previously. I encourage him to extend his thinking further, paraphrasing the information in the text that answers his questions about how old the pyramids are.

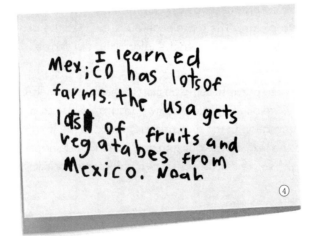

4 Noah, a more experienced reader, pretty much restated the information in the text. This is fine for a start, but I would encourage him to read a more sophisticated text independently because he is ready to apply paraphrasing skills in more challenging text.

Independent Practice Post-its

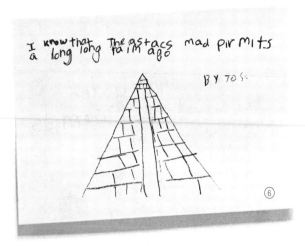

"It took them a very long time to build it but they built it."

"I know that the Aztecs made pyramids a long time ago."

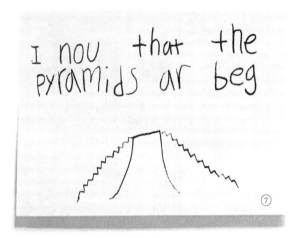

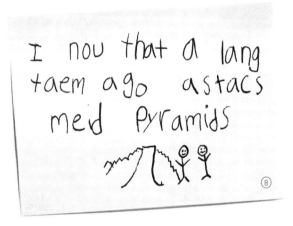

"I know the pyramids are big."

"I know that a long time ago Aztecs made pyramids."

5–8 Jaime (5 and 6) and Lizette (7 and 8) are native Spanish speakers who are learning English. Their thinking contains background knowledge and information they had learned from a study of Mexico, which they shared orally during a conference. They then wrote these Post-its on their own. Their ability to merge their thinking with information in the text shows the important role background knowledge plays in reading and understanding information. Both Jaime and Lizette were excited to contribute to the discussion and teach their peers what they knew about the Aztecs.

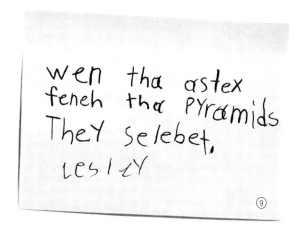

"When the Aztecs finished the pyramid, they cele-brated."

"Pyramids are different shapes and different sizes."

"The pryamids have been invented by Aztecs."

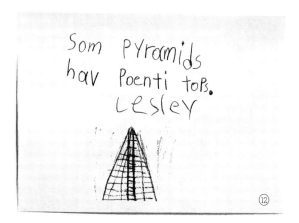

"Some pyramids have pointy tops."

9–12 Lesley, an English Language Learner of Mexican heritage, had extensive knowledge about the pyramids, which she was excited to share. We believe there's no better way for kids to learn a new language than drawing and writing about what they know. Lesley's voice and background knowledge come through loud and clear in her Post-its. She spent a long time drawing and writing these, and she demonstrates how prolific young children can be when they are truly engaged.

Second-Grade Response

13 For more developed readers, paraphrasing becomes a tool for learning and recording information. More developed readers use paraphrasing in their own research. This child compared tigers and jaguars for a large poster she created about big cats. She merged her thinking with the information, reacting to the amazing information she read. Her work became an example other kids could learn from as she shared how she put the information into her own words. Most important, her curiosity, enthusiasm, and voice come through loud and clear.

Paraphrase Information

Merge your thinking to make meaning

TEACHING MOVES	TEACHING LANGUAGE
	Connect and Engage
Review that when learners read for information, they read, stop, and think about it.	■ Let's remember that one of the best ways to learn new information is to look carefully, stop for a moment, and think about it.
	■ Take a look at these pictures. Then turn and talk about what you observe and have learned from them.
Reiterate some of the strategies kids use to get information from photographs.	■ You are using some good strategies for making sense of this information. You looked carefully at the…and learned from them. Some of you added your background knowledge. You activated it and made connections to the information.
Remind kids to pay special attention to the nonfiction features.	■ Another thing you did to make sense of the information was to pay attention to features, like this….
	Model
Introduce and define the term *paraphrase*.	■ I'm going to read the information and then say what I learned in my own words. When we say something in our own words, we call it *paraphrasing*.
List the steps of paraphrasing information.	■ I've written the steps for paraphrasing here. First, read the information, stop, and think about it. Next, say the information in your own words, but don't say too much. Then, react and respond to the information, merging your thinking with it.
Model how to paraphrase and record your thinking, merging your thinking with the information.	■ Let's try this. I'm going to read this information and then think about it in order to put it in my own words.
	■ On the left side of this chart, I'll write the information that I'm reading about. Then I'll think about the information, put it in my own words, and write it on the right-hand side.
	■ So I'll say…and write it on the left. Now I'm thinking about all the information, and I'm adding my own ideas to it. I'll merge my thinking with the information and write it here.

The Teaching Moves outline your instructional sequence and the
Teaching Language gives you an idea about what to say to your students.

TEACHING LANGUAGE	TEACHING MOVES

Guide

- Work with a partner to put information in your own words and add your thinking to it. Write it on Post-its and then we'll share out in a few minutes.

  Continue reading, and then ask kids to turn and talk to try to put the information in their own words.

- Let's add your thinking to the *Paraphrasing* Anchor Chart. As you share, I'll write the words from the text on the left. I'll write your paraphrased information on the right. Who would like to share?

  Invite kids to share out their thinking and record it on the Anchor Chart.

- Tell us some more about… That's an important connection you've made. Let me add your thinking to the Anchor Chart.

  Expand on a comment from one child to show how to merge thinking with the information and paraphrase.

Collaborate or Practice Independently

- Now you are going to try this on your own. You can use this same material or any book you choose. When you come to some important information, stop and think about it, put it in your own words, and add a reaction if you'd like. Look up at the chart if you need a reminder.

  Send kids off to read and put information into their own words, reminding them to look at the chart if they need guidance.

- I will come around and confer as you work. Make sure you are merging your thinking with the information.

  Confer with kids to make sure they have accurate information and are merging their thinking with the information.

Share the Learning

- Who chose a different book? Would you like to share…? You really thought about this information! And you didn't tell too much….

  Invite kids who selected the lesson text and other nonfiction text to share their experience with paraphrasing and adding personal reactions.

- You have done a fine job of reading and viewing to learn new information and then put it in your own words! You have really shaped your learning into a new thought! Remember to use the Anchor Chart as a guide!

  Wrap up the lesson and remind children to use the Anchor Chart as a guide to paraphrasing information.

Reflect & Assess

Did your students:

- stop and think about new information they learned from their reading?
- put information in their own words and shape their learning into a new thought?
- react, respond, and merge their thinking with the information to better remember it?

Organize Your Thinking as You Re

Text Matters

In this lesson, we teach kids to take their own notes while reading accessible texts. As always, we make sure that the classroom contains plenty of nonfiction on all sorts of interesting topics. A range of reading levels allows kids to choose an appropriate book. Choice makes a big difference. Kids are eager to learn about and investigate topics they are interested in, and clear, engaging texts are just what beginning note-takers need. In the classroom, we have books, magazines, and even Internet articles at a variety of different reading levels and with a plethora of photographs and features to ensure that all kids view, read, and respond to new information.

Resources & Materials

Lesson Text
TIME For Kids Bigger Picture Edition [Spring 2003] "Welcome to the Rain Forest" poster

Additional Texts
Nonfiction texts on various topics and a range of visual and text features

Classroom Supplies
- *I Learned/I Wonder/Wow!* Anchor Chart
- Marker

Student Supplies
- Student copy of "Welcome to the Rain Forest" [See *Keep Reading! A Source Book of Short Text*, pages 21–24, or the DVD-ROM.]
- *I Learned/I Wonder/Wow!* Thinksheet [See *Strategy Book 5*, page 51, or the DVD-ROM.]
- Clipboard with pencil and Post-its or Post-its Thinksheets [See *Strategy Book 5*, pages 52–53, or the DVD-ROM.]

Take notes to record information

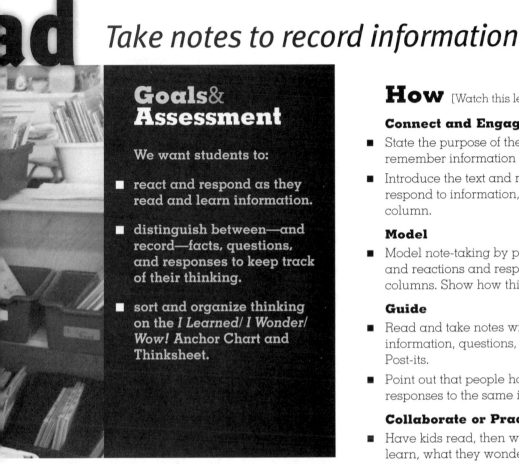

Goals & Assessment

We want students to:

- **react and respond as they read and learn information.**

- **distinguish between—and record—facts, questions, and responses to keep track of their thinking.**

- **sort and organize thinking on the *I Learned/ I Wonder/ Wow!* Anchor Chart and Thinksheet.**

How [Watch this lesson on the *PTK* DVD-ROM.]

Connect and Engage

- State the purpose of the lesson: Taking notes to remember information and organize thinking.

- Introduce the text and review how we react and respond to information, recording it in the *Wow!* column.

Model

- Model note-taking by putting information, questions, and reactions and responses in the appropriate columns. Show how thinking connects across columns.

Guide

- Read and take notes with kids. Guide them to write information, questions, and reactions and responses on Post-its.

- Point out that people have different reactions and responses to the same information.

Collaborate or Practice Independently

- Have kids read, then write and/or draw what they learn, what they wonder, and their response.

- Pull together a small group and show them how to sort Post-its on the *I Learned/I Wonder/Wow!* Thinksheet.

Share the Learning

- Invite kids to share how they sorted and organized their thinking and then put Post-its in the appropriate column on the chart.

- Pass out individual thinksheets for kids to continue their sorting work on.

Why & What

Young children revel in facts and details about things that interest them. They naturally respond, exclaiming "Amazing!," "I never knew that!," or "Cool!". We want them to *remember* what they have learned and here we teach kids a process for taking notes that involves more than "just the facts." We teach kids to record, sort, and organize their newfound information. Sometimes a question follows hot on the heels of new learning or kids react to startling information. We show kids how facts, questions, and responses are related using the *I Learned/I Wonder/Wow!* chart and Thinksheet. This note-taking scaffold provides a format for kids to write, draw, and collect new knowledge. Their notes and thinksheets provide a record of their evolving thinking.

The rain forest is one of the most colorful habitats in the world. From the ground to the treetops, it is bursting with living things.

Lesson Text

The *TFK* "Welcome to the Rain Forest" poster contains information that is appropriately organized for beginning note-takers. The separate sections on different rain forest animals encourage kids to notice new learning and prompt their questions, reactions, and responses. Each section contains a manageable amount of information and makes it easy for kids to take notes on Post-its and organize their thinking. While some kids continue to read, learn from, and respond to the poster for the duration of the lesson, other children choose other accessible nonfiction texts and use this same format for recording their thinking. When kids choose books that they are enthusiastic about, they are more likely to read to learn on their own, inside and outside of school.

Used with permission from *Time For Kids*.

TEACHING MOVES	TEACHING LANGUAGE

Connect and Engage

State the purpose of the lesson: Taking notes to remember information and organize thinking.

We're going to learn to take notes today. But we're going to do more than write down just the facts. As we read, we will write down what we learn, what we wonder, and our reactions to information. When we want to investigate a topic that interests us, we take notes. We read the text, view the pictures, and write down what we are learning to keep track of it. If we have good notes, we can use them to write and illustrate our learning so we can share it with others.

When we read today, we'll be using a chart with columns that should look familiar. *[I point to* I Learned/I Wonder/Wow! *Anchor Chart.]* We've spent a lot of time learning facts and new information. That's what goes in the first column labeled *I Learned*. You all love to ask questions. We record our questions in the *I Wonder* column. Now let's look at the column entitled *Wow!* When we say "Wow!" or "Amazing!" or "Cool!" we are reacting and responding to information. Remember a reaction or response is something we think or feel about the information we're learning—or it can be a connection to our background knowledge or experience.

Introduce the text and review how we react and respond to information, recording it in the *Wow!* column.

Let's take a look at this poster about the rain forest. *[I have tacked up the* "Welcome to the Rain Forest" *poster on the board.]* It's called "Welcome to the Rain Forest" so I know we will be reading about the rain forest. Do any of you have reactions or responses to this photograph?

Javier: That's one big toucan!

Zoe: I know toucans eat figs. There was a picture of one throwing a fig up in the air and catching it with its beak!

Oliver: I had an encounter with a toucan. One was trying to peck my brother's backpack. My mom shooed it away.

Such interesting responses and reactions! I'll write these responses in the *Wow!* column of the Anchor Chart. I agree with Javier. That's a big bird! And Oliver, that's such an interesting word: *encounter*. An encounter is often a special experience; you had an experience with a toucan.

Oliver: It was pecking my brother's backpack!

That's a pretty exciting encounter, I'd say!

Can you visualize Oliver having an encounter with a toucan in the middle of a rain forest?

Now picture Zoe's description of a toucan throwing a fig in the air and catching it with its beak. How great that we have some interesting responses in the *Wow!* column—remember that's where we write reactions, responses, connections, and even stuff we already know, our background knowledge.

This chart will help us keep all our thinking straight! I'm thinking that this poster is about animals that live in the rain forest. Let's see what we can learn about them. You've already shared your reactions as well as some of your background knowledge about toucans.

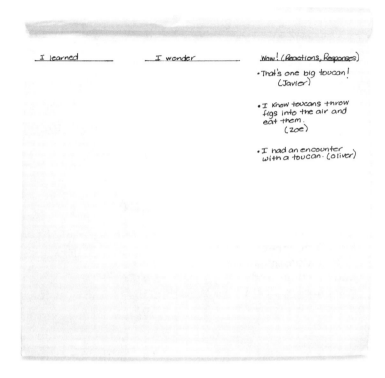

Model

I'm going to write facts in the first column and questions in the *I Wonder* column. I already took some notes in the *Wow!* column—that's where I wrote down Javier's, Zoe's, and Oliver's reactions and responses.

Now I'm going to show you how I look at this cover photograph and learn from it. I have a reaction to this photo. Remember we can use words like "Wow" to react to information. I'm going to say I'm amazed that the toucan has such a huge beak! I'll write this in the *Wow!* column. *[I write it on the Anchor Chart as I talk.]* That huge beak made me think of a question: "I wonder how the toucan flies with such a giant beak." I'll write my question in the *I Wonder* column and sketch the toucan right here to show that big beak. And then I'll draw an arrow to connect my question to my reaction.

Turn and talk for a minute. Did you learn anything from the photograph? Do you have any questions? Or maybe you have a response or a reaction.

Janeth: Look at that tiny frog up there in the corner. It's only as big as a fingernail.

Jeremiah: I wonder if a frog that little is a poison frog.

TIP: We begin the lesson with reactions and responses to highlight these. Kids have had a great deal of practice with "I learned" and "I wonder," so we emphasize reactions that we record in the *Wow!* column.

Model note-taking by putting information, questions, and reactions and responses in the appropriate columns. Show how thinking connects across columns.

Janeth, you were paying really close attention to the photograph up in the corner. I think we all learned something from the picture of this tiny frog, which you said is only as big as a fingernail! Let's write what you learned, Janeth. *[I write Some frogs are tiny—only as big as a fingernail!]* Then I'm going to draw a frog about that size—just to show how small it really is. And then we can write down Jeremiah's question—well, where, Jeremiah?

Jeremiah: Write it in the *I Wonder* column.

Exactly—right next to the information about the tiny frog. *[I write Is this little frog poisonous?]* Before we go on, I want you to notice how our thinking connects across columns. Just now, Jeremiah had a question about the information that Janeth shared. He wondered if that little frog is poisonous—so we use an arrow to connect Jeremiah's question to the information in the *I Learned* column.

Guide

Read and take notes with kids. Guide them to write information, questions, and reactions and responses on Post-its.

I think you are ready to listen, read, and view as we go on to learn more about rain forest animals. Let's do some reading and take notes together. *[I hand out the clipboards, pencils, and Post-its.]* As I read, I'd like you to write and draw your thinking on the Post-its and I'll write our notes up on the Anchor Chart.

[I read "The Forest Roof..."] So the canopy is part of the rain forest—it's high up in the trees and all the animals we'll be reading about live there. Let's read about the forest roof and then these blue frogs that we see in the photo:

> Some animals stand out. The color of these frogs sends a warning. It says, "Watch out!" The frogs have poison.

Now go ahead and look carefully at the photograph and think about the information I just read. Then turn and talk about what you learned, what you wonder, or a reaction you have.

Bergen: I saw a blue frog before . . . I know frogs in the rain forest are all different colors.

You could write that on a Post-it, Bergen. You have some background knowledge, and we could put that in the *Wow!* column. *[I write Bergen's thought in the Wow! column.]* I'm surprised there are blue frogs. I'll write my reaction on the chart, too. *[I write I'm surprised! There are blue frogs!]*

Point out that people have different reactions and responses to the same information.

Did you notice that Bergen and I had different responses to the same information? I was surprised that frogs can be blue. But Bergen already knew there are frogs of many colors, so she had a different reaction. People can have different responses to the same information. That's what's so great—people think differently from each other, and that makes discussing our thinking so interesting! And we can't forget to write the information we're reacting to in the *I Learned* column. I'll write *Bright blue frogs are poisonous* and connect what we learned to our reactions with an arrow.

I learned	I wonder	Wow! (Reactions, Responses)

• That's one big toucan! (Javier)

• I know toucans throw figs into the air and eat them. (Zoe)

• I had an encounter with a toucan. (Oliver)

• I wonder how the toucan flies with such a giant beak. ⟵ • I'm amazed that the toucan has such a huge beak!

• Some frogs are tiny— only as big as a fingernail! → • Is this little frog poisonous? •I know frogs in the rainforest are all different colors.

• Bright blue frogs are poisonous. • I'm surprised! There are blue frogs!

Collaborate or Practice Independently

Have kids read, then write and/or draw what they learn, what they wonder, and their response.

I think you are ready to take notes on your own Post-its. You can work by yourself or with a partner. You can use the small version of the *TFK* rain forest poster or choose a book from the baskets around the room. Keep on taking notes—writing and drawing what you learn, what you wonder, and your reactions and responses. Remember, you can learn information by looking at the pictures and features and by reading the words.

As you write on your Post-its, remember to write just one fact, question, or response on each. You can also code your thinking—you can write an *L* for *learned*, a *?* for a question, and an *!* for Wow!

Pull together a small group and show them how to sort Post-its on the *I Learned/I Wonder/Wow!* Thinksheet.

TIP: Teaching and discussing how to sort and categorize Post-its is much more effective with a small group than trying to do this with 25 kids all at once!

[As kids work in pairs or independently, I gather a small group of children who have written several Post-its and we work together to sort their Post-its into columns on their individual I Learned/I Wonder/Wow! *Thinksheets.]*

Share the Learning

Invite kids to share how they sorted and organized their thinking and then put Post-its in the appropriate column on the chart.

[To wrap up the lesson, we come together and a few kids share their Post-its. Other kids share how they sorted their Post-its on their individual I Learned/I Wonder/ Wow! *Thinksheets.]*

Let's share out what you learned, or something you wondered, or maybe you want to tell us about your response.

Ezekiel: I drew a jaguar. I learned jaguars have spots and whiskers and little ears.

This is a beautiful drawing of a jaguar. How about if we put it up on the Anchor Chart in the *I Learned* column? We learned a lot about what a jaguar looks like from your illustration: its spots, its color, and even what the ears look like! You took time to draw this accurately and carefully.

Who else would like to share?

Briana: I had a question. *[She reads her Post-it.]* "I wonder if there are frogs in the rain forest?"

And you have another Post-it. What does it say?

Briana: I had an answer. I wrote, "I learned that tree frogs live in the rain forest."

Briana has an *L* for what she *learned* on one Post-it and also an *A* on her other Post-it because that is the *answer* to her question. And you can see she drew an arrow from her question to her answer, to show us how she connected her thinking. Thank you so much, Briana, for teaching us how to put a code on our Post-its and connect our thinking!

Now I'd like Frankie to share how he sorted his Post-its, putting them in columns on the *I Learned/I Wonder/Wow!* Thinksheet.

Frankie: First I put all my *I Learneds* in the *I Learned* column. I had a lot of 'em! Then I had some questions. I really wondered if you touch a poison dart frog, will you die?

That's an interesting question—tell us about your *Wow!'s*—your reactions and responses.

Frankie: I didn't have any, but then I thought "Sloths can climb trees." I was really surprised because I never knew that. I put it in the *Wow!* column.

You learned a lot. You had some questions and you responded to some surprising information, Frankie—great job.

[I hand out I Learned/I Wonder/Wow! *Thinksheets.]* Now it's your turn to sort your Post-its on this thinksheet. Then you can keep track of your thinking as you learn new information, ask questions, and respond. Have fun sorting!

Pass out individual thinksheets for kids to continue their sorting work on.

Did your students:

- react and respond as they read and learned information?

- distinguish between—and record—facts, questions, and responses to keep track of their thinking?

- sort and organize thinking on the *I Learned/ I Wonder/ Wow!* Anchor Chart and Thinksheet?

Reflect& Assess

To assess how well students understand the *I Learned/I Wonder/Wow!* note-taking strategy, we look at their Post-its and thinksheets on which they have begun to sort and organize their Post-its. We look for information written in their own words, questions that follow from the information, and authentic responses and reactions that reveal connections to prior knowledge that helped kids understand what they were reading. During collaborative practice, I pull small groups of kids to assess how well they are able to use the "I Learned, I Wonder, Wow!" language and if they are clear about the difference between facts, questions, and responses. I then introduce the *I Learned/I Wonder/Wow!* Thinksheet, helping children sort their Post-its into the correct columns. The *I Learned/I Wonder/Wow!* Anchor Chart provides a place for kids to begin to sort and organize their Post-its. Kids are then able to take a step back and notice all the great thinking and learning they are creating!

Adapt& Differentiate

This lesson was done with first graders, but here are suggestions for how to adapt and differentiate for the whole range of learners.

Sorting and organizing thinking on a scaffold like the *I Learned/I Wonder/Wow!* Thinksheet makes sense once kids clearly understand and can discriminate among facts and information, questions, and reactions and responses. With very young children, the teaching emphasis would be on understanding the difference between a fact and a question. Then we would bring in responses and reactions and practice writing down our thinking and putting it up on an *I Learned/ I Wonder/Wow!* Anchor Chart.

More experienced students who have considerable practice with taking notes in this format begin to use this scaffold as a tool for research. As they investigate their own topics, kids spontaneously organize their thinking and Post-its into columns or take notes directly on the thinksheet. Many children use the chart/thinksheet as a place to gather and review their new learning, and others create posters using these columns to synthesize their evolving thinking (see the Assessment example in Lesson 21).

First-Grade Responses

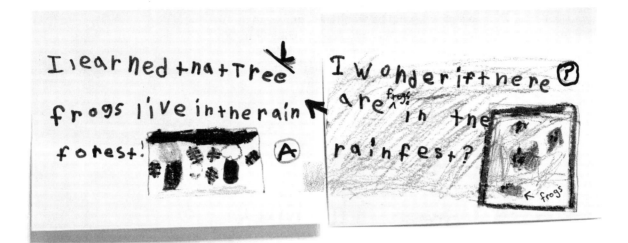

1 Briana shared her thinking during the lesson. Her Post-its with her question and answer showed kids how she connected her question to her answer with an arrow. Briana teaches the rest of the class how to code their thinking with a ? to denote her question and an A to denote her answer. Kids pay attention when a peer becomes the teacher!

2 This student learned that some frogs are the size of a fingernail and illustrated this comparison—connecting his picture of the frog to the picture of a fingernail with an arrow. I encourage kids to use all manner of features because they are such an important way to visually communicate information.

3 This student's illustration adds so much to his thinking. As kids grow older, we find they are less inclined to illustrate their thinking with remarkable artwork such as this. So we try to remind ourselves that drawing and illustrating are powerful ways to represent and share information, no matter what the age!

4 An English Language Learner, Frankie's enthusiasm for finding out new information is contagious. In just a short time, he worked independently to jot down what he learned, what he wondered, and even a Wow! Frankie did a great job of writing down as much as he could, but his oral explanations were more complete than what he was able to get down in writing. He came to the small group lesson and learned quickly how to sort and organize his Post-its on the thinksheet.

Rain Forest Thinking

I learned

I learned that snake eat Lisht

I learned that taas Some Pramos

I learned that thas Some Froeg in the rine forste hav Pousin

I wonder

I wonder if hirrs green boas

I wonder how kast ths the Slof go

I wonder if you tosh a Pousin don't krog you well died

Wow!

wow Slof coh camb trees.

"I learned that snakes eat lizards."

"I learned there are piranhas."

"I learned that some frogs in the rain forest have poison."

"I wonder if there are green boas."

"I wonder how fast the sloth goes."

"I wonder if you touch a poison dart frog, will you die?"

"Wow! Sloths can climb trees!"

5 Zoe left traces of her thinking as she read and viewed the "Welcome to the Rain Forest" poster. She recorded information about katydids and their spikey legs. She also had a question: "I wonder how many species of insects are in the world?" I talked with her about the meaning of the word *species*, and we discussed how she could begin to investigate it, knowing that the question might have many different answers, depending on the source she consults. She also found a fact she reacted to and added it to her chart.

"I learned that katydids have spikes on (their) legs!"

"I wonder how many species of insects (there are) in the world?"

"Wow, I didn't know a leaf beetle larva protects it(self) with its own droppings! Gross!"

6 Brenda has lots of thinking going on. She is learning information, asking questions, and responding. Her sorted Post-its demonstrate her understanding of the distinctions between facts, questions, and responses even though one question ended up in the *Wow!* column. Her arrow across columns demonstrates that she is connecting what she learns with what she wonders.

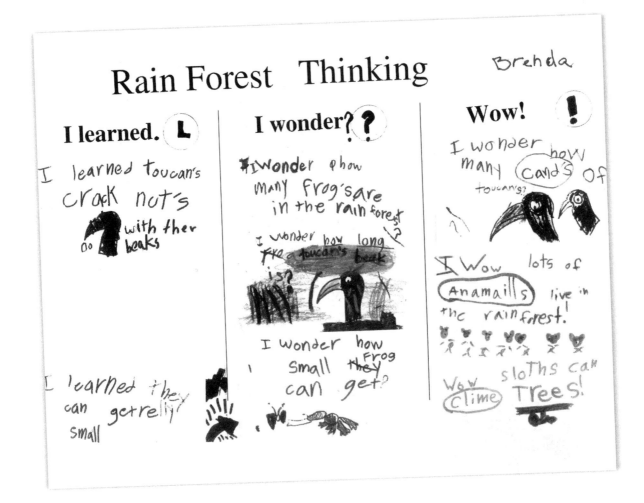

Second-Grade Response

7 This second-grade student created a poster using the *I Learned/ I Wonder/Wow!* scaffold. She organized and illustrated information, demonstrating how this note-taking scaffold becomes a tool for gathering and expressing thinking and new learning.

Organize Your Thinking as You Read

Take notes to record information

TEACHING MOVES	TEACHING LANGUAGE
	Connect and Engage
State the purpose of the lesson: Taking notes to remember information and organize thinking.	■ As we read today, we are going to take notes on what we learn, what we wonder, and our response. If we have good notes, we can use them to write and illustrate our learning. Then we can share our learning with others.
	■ We will be using the *I Learned/I Wonder/Wow!* Anchor Chart to sort and organize our thinking and learning.
Introduce the text and review how we react and respond to information, recording it in the *Wow!* column.	■ Let's take a look at this. Do you have reactions or responses to it? How great that we have so many great responses in the *Wow!* column—that's where we write reaction, responses, connections, and even stuff we already know. A reaction or a response is something we think or feel about the information we're learning.
	Model
Model note-taking by putting information, questions, and reactions and responses in the appropriate columns. Show how thinking connects across columns.	■ Notice how I write facts in the first column, questions in the second column, and reactions and responses in the third column.
	■ I'm going to show you how I take notes. I have a reaction to…. I'm going to write *I'm amazed…*in the *Wow!* column. That makes me wonder something. I'm going to write my question in the *I Wonder* column.
	■ We can even draw an arrow from the information to our question or our response because they are connected.
	Guide
Read and take notes with kids. Guide them to write information, questions, and reactions and responses on Post-its.	■ Let's do some reading and take notes together. As I read, I'd like you to write and draw your thinking on Post-its.
	■ Now, turn and talk about what you learned, what you wonder, or a reaction you have. Who learned some things? Who has a question? Who has a reaction? I have a reaction, too. Let's write them in the *Wow!* column.
Point out that people have different reactions and responses to the same information.	■ Did you notice that…and I had different responses to the same information? Isn't that cool? It makes it so interesting to discuss our thinking!

The Teaching Moves outline your instructional sequence and the
Teaching Language gives you an idea about what to say to your students.

TEACHING LANGUAGE	TEACHING MOVES

Collaborate or Practice Independently

- Now you can try this on your own or work with a partner. You can continue to use the…we have been reading together or you can choose another book or article. Keep on taking notes—drawing and writing what you learn, what you wonder, and your reactions and responses.

Have kids read, then write and/or draw what they learn, what they wonder, and their response.

- Let's try sorting your Post-its on the *I Learned/I Wonder/Wow!* Thinksheet. I'll come around to confer with you as you try this.

Pull together a small group and show them how to sort Post-its on the *I Learned/I Wonder/Wow!* Thinksheet.

Share the Learning

- Who would like to share something you learned, something you wondered, or your response to some information?

Invite kids to share how they sorted and organized their thinking and then put Post-its in the appropriate column on the chart.

- *[Kids share various responses.]* We learned a lot from your illustration…now we know how to sort our Post-its.

- Use this thinksheet to keep track of your thinking and organize it as you learn new information, ask questions, and respond.

Pass out individual thinksheets for kids to continue their sorting work on.

Reflect & Assess

Did your students:
- react and respond as they read and learned information?
- distinguish between—and record—facts, questions, and responses to keep track of their thinking?
- sort and organize thinking on the *I Learned/ I Wonder/ Wow!* Anchor Chart and Thinksheet?

Determine Importance Strategy Wrap-up:
Creating an Anchor Chart to Capture What We Learned about Determining Importance

Teaching Language

Now that we have done some lessons on determining what's important when we read, listen, and view, let's take a look back at what we have learned. We can co-construct an Anchor Chart about this strategy that will serve as a visual reminder of ways we can pick out the most important information and organize it to make sense of it.

I'll begin by sharing something I do when I choose the most important information, and I will record it on the chart. For instance, when I'm trying to pick out the most important information, I have to distinguish between the interesting details and the important information. After I jot this down, we'll talk about other ways we decide what's important.

[Whenever possible, we want to capture kids' comments that show their understanding of the strategy as well as our lesson language to guide future teaching and learning.]

What We Learned about Determining Importance

We learn to tell the difference between interesting details and important information.

We put a star by the most important information as we read. We call this coding our thinking.

We paraphrase important information. That means we put the information into our own words so we really understand it.

We review the difference between facts, questions, and responses. We learn to take notes—recording facts, asking questions, and reacting and responding to what we learn.

We take notes to keep track of and organize our thinking. This helps us get ready to share it with others.

Assessment Checklist for Determine Importance

Expectations for student thinking and learning

- Distinguish between interesting details and important information to help determine what to learn and remember
- Code the text with a star to identify what's important
- Paraphrase important information to put the information into our own words so we better understand it
- Distinguish between facts, questions, and responses as we take notes

Questions you can ask yourself to assess student understanding

- Are they able to separate interesting details from the more important information so they can remember it?
- Can they pick out important information and code it with a star?
- Can they paraphrase information, putting what's most important into their own words—orally and, if appropriate, through writing and drawing?
- Can they distinguish between facts, questions, and responses?
- Can they sort and organize their learning as they take notes to keep track of their thinking?

Language of determining importance

"This is really important…"

"This is important to remember…"

"I think this might be important…"

"I think this part means…"

"This information makes me think…"

Language of facts, questions, and responses

"I learned, I wonder, WOW!"

"Amazing!"

"I think…"

"I feel…"

"I have a connection…"

"My background knowledge tells me…"

Annotated Rubric for Strategy Book 5: Determine Importance

Name _____   Date _____

Oral and/or Written Evidence	Strong Evidence 3		Some Evidence 2		Little Evidence 1
Distinguishes between what are interesting details and what is important information					
Identifies and codes important information					
Paraphrases, putting information into own words to better understand it					
Distinguishes between facts, questions, responses in taking notes					
Organizes thinking to prepare to share it					

© 2008 by Stephanie Harvey and Anne Goudvis from *The Primary Comprehension Toolkit*. Portsmouth, NH: Heinemann. This page may be photocopied for classroom use only.

Name _____   Date _____

Wow!	
I Wonder	
I Learned	

© 2008 by Stephanie Harvey and Anne Goudvis from *The Primary Comprehension Toolkit* Portsmouth, NH: Heinemann. This page may be photocopied for classroom use only.

Name _____   Date _____

© 2008 by Stephanie Harvey and Anne Goudvis from *The Primary Comprehension Toolkit*
Portsmouth, NH: Heinemann. This page may be photocopied for classroom use only.

Name _____ Date _____

© 2008 by Stephanie Harvey and Anne Goudvis from *The Primary Comprehension Toolkit*
Portsmouth, NH: Heinemann. This page may be photocopied for classroom use only.